MAY 9 - JUNE 30, 1995

PICASSO

MASTERWORKS · 1903–1969

RICHARD GRAY
GALLERY

SUITE 2503 / JOHN HANCOCK CENTER

875 NORTH MICHIGAN AVENUE, CHICAGO, ILLINOIS 60611

TEL. 312/642-8877 · FAX 312/642-8488

Pablo Picasso is widely acknowledged to be the twentieth century's most influential artist. Outside forces have played a central role in his own work, with much inspiration drawn from ancient and primitive cultures, other periods and traditions in art. In turn few western artists of distinction in our century have remained free from the stimuli of Picasso's invention and synthesis of these other ideas.

A multitude of publications and exhibitions have been produced exploring Picasso's range and authority as an artist. No one involved in any way with the visual arts can fail to be touched by his genius.

With my own gradual discovery of the depth and complexity in Picasso's work and during my thirty years as a dealer in modern art, it has been an ever present influence. It informs my aesthetic judgments, affecting decisions on what is of interest and what we will show. In considering an appropriate exhibition to inaugurate our new premises, I could think of no other artist whose breadth of expressions and level of accomplishment so commands my continued attention. I am pleased to present this exhibition which includes so many singular examples of major phases of Picasso's production.

The works that have been assembled are drawn from a variety of sources, mostly distinguished private collections. Many have passed through our hands before. The cooperation and generosity of the lenders is gratefully acknowledged.

RICHARD GRAY

1. **Femme et Enfant au bord de la Mer** 1902–1903

Pastel on paper

18.11" x 12.2" · 46 x 31 cm

Signed lower left in black chalk

PROVENANCE

Mme. Besnard, Paris (1903)
Paul Rosenberg, Paris
George Halphen, Paris (June 8, 1936)
Richard Gray Gallery, Chicago
Private Collection, USA

EXHIBITED

Zurich, Kunsthaus, "Picasso", 1932, #272.

Quimper, Musée des Beaux Arts, "Max Jacob et Picasso",
June 21–November 15, 1994; Paris, Musée Picasso,
November 30, 1994–February 6, 1995.

LITERATURE

Daix, Pierre and Georges Boudaille, *Picasso: The
Blue and Rose Period: 1900–1906*, vol. VII. 21,
New York Graphic Society, Ltd., Connecticut,
1966–1968; Editions Ides et Calendes, Neuchâtel,
1966 and 1988, ill. p. 212.

Cassou, Jean, *Picasso*, The Hyperion Press, Paris,
1940, ill. p. 52.

Richardson, John, *A Life of Picasso*, Vol. I, 1881–1906,
1991, ill. p. 266.

Zervos, Christian, *Pablo Picasso: Oeuvres de 1895 a 1906*,
Vol. I, Edition Cahiers d'Art, Paris, p. 184, #381.

"If Picasso's first three visits to Paris all ended shortly before or after Christmas, this can be attributed to his Andalusian loathing of the cold. Why go on freezing and starving when he could return home to Barcelona and the relative comfort of his parent's apartment? The main problem in January 1903 was money for the ticket home. Picasso was not going to apply to his family as he had done last time. Berthe Weill claimed to be broke, so Picasso threw himself on the mercy of Madame Besnard, the wife of his color merchant, who already had a small collection of his work. Madame Besnard was persuaded to pay two hundred francs for the superb pastel Mother and Child on the Shore that he had brought with him from Barcelona to sell at the December show." (Richardson, p. 266)

2. **Femme Nue Debout** 1906

Pencil on paper
12.5" x 9.2" · 32 x 23 cm

PROVENANCE

The Artist
Gertrude Stein, Paris
George E. Seligmann, New York
Private Collection, New York
Acquavella Galleries, Inc., New York
Richard and Mary L. Gray, Chicago

EXHIBITION

New York, The Museum of Modern Art, "Four Americans
in Paris, The Collection of Gertrude Stein & Family",
December 19, 1970–January 31, 1971, p. 168.

Basel, Galerie Beyeler, "Nudes-Nus-Nackte", June–August,
1984, #58.

Basel, Galerie Beyeler, "Picasso: der Maler und seine
Modelle", July–October, 1986, ill. p. 11, #62.

LITERATURE

Zervos, Christian, *Pablo Picasso, Oeuvres: Supplément aux
volumes 1 à 5*, Vol. VI, p. 107, #886.

3. **Torse de Femme** 1908

Gouache on paper
24.63" x 18.75" · 63 x 48 cm

Signed upper right

LITERATURE

Brettel, Richard R., *An Impressionist Legacy: The Collection of
Sara Lee Corporation*, Abbeville Press, New York, 1990, ill. in
color pp. 54 & 55.

Daix, Pierre and Joan Rosselet, *Picasso: The Cubist Years
1907–1916*, Thames and Hudson, London, 1979, ill. p. 211.

Fry, Edward, *Cubism*, Oxford University Press,
New York, 1966.

Pablo Picasso: A Retrospective, The Museum of Modern Art,
New York, 1980.

"Resisting Cezanne: Picasso's 'Three Woman'", *Art in
America*, vol. 66, November/December 1978, pp. 114–33.

Rubin, Willaim, "Picasso", In "Primitivism", *20th Century
Art: Affinity of the Tribal and the Modern*, Vol. I, The
Museum of Modern Art, 1984, pp. 240–343.

Russoli, Franco and Fiorella Minervino, *L'Opera comlpeta
di Picasso cubista*, Rizzoli Editore, Milan, 1972, p. 93.

Selections from the Nathan Cummings Collection, National
Gallery of Art, Washington, D.C., 1970, p. 52.

Zervos, Christian, *Pablo Picasso: Oeuvres de 1906 à 1916*,
Vol II, part I, Editions Cahiers d'Art, Paris, p. 30, #57.

4. **Couseuse** 1910

Oil on canvas

31.5" x 23.25" · 80 x 60 cm

Signed upper left

PROVENANCE

Curt Valentine, New York
Newhouse Galleries, New York, 1937
Walter P. Chrysler, Jr., New York, 1937
Claire Zeisler, Chicago

EXHIBITED

Chicago, The Art Institute of Chicago, "Picasso in Chicago:
Paintings, Drawings and Prints from Chicago Collections",
February 3 – March 31, 1968.

New York, The Museum of Modern Art, "Picasso and
Braque Pioneering Cubism", September 1989–January 1990

LITERATURE

Daix, Pierre, *Picasso, The Cubist Years 1907–1916*, New York
Graphic Society, Boston, 1979, ill. p. 252, #331.

"Picasso in Chicago: Paintings, Drawings and Prints from
Chicago Collections", Art Institute of Chicago, 1968,
ill. p. 20, #13.

Rubin, William, *Picasso and Braque: Pioneering Cubism*,
The Museum of Modern Art, Little, Brown and Co.,
Boston, 1989, ill. in color p. 152.

Zervos, Christian, *Pablo Picasso, Oeuvres de 1906–1912*, Vol. II,
Part 1, Edition Cahiers d'Art, Paris, p. 99, #199.

5. **Violin** Autumn, 1912

Collage with charcoal and watercolor,
with traces of blue gouache, on ivory
laid paper.

24.5" x 18.8" · 62.5 x 48 cm

Signed on reverse

PROVENANCE

Galerie Kahnweiler, Paris, (archive photo no. 291)
Tristan Tzara, Paris
The New Gallery, New York
E.V. Thaw & Co., New York
Mr. & Mrs. James W. Alsdorf, Chicago
Alsdorf Foundation, Chicago

EXHIBITED

Paris, Galeries Georges Petit, "Picasso", Retrospective
1901–1932, July 16–July 30, 1932, catalogue by Charles
Vrancken. #82 (?).

Zurich, Kunsthaus, "Picasso", Retrospective 1901–1932
with the bulk of the works from the Paris 1932 exhibition.
September 11–October 30 (extended to November 13),
1932, catalogue by Charles Vrancken and W. Wartmann,
#72 (?).

New York, The New Gallery, "10th Anniversary Exhibition", September 14–October 31, 1959, catalogue #18, rep.
on the cover.

New York, Cooperating New York Galleries, "Picasso: An
American Tribute", April 25–May, 1962, catalogue by John
Richardson, exhibition organized jointly by nine New York
galleries including M. Knoedler & Co. (1895–1909),
Saidenberg Gallery (Cubism), Duveen Brothers, Inc. (The
Classic Phase), and The New Gallery (Drawings), ill. #12.

Tokyo, National Museum of Modern Art, "Master Drawings by Picasso", Retrospective 1899–1970, May 23– July 5,
1964. The exhibition also traveled to: Kyoto, National
Museum of Modern Art, July 10–August 2, 1964; Nagoya,
Prefectural Museum of Art, August 7–August 18, 1964,
catalogue ill. #23.

LITERATURE

Daix, Pierre and Joan Rosselet, *Picasso: The Cubist Years,
1907–1916*, New York Graphic Society, Boston, 1979,
ill. p. 290, #525.

Rubin, William, *Picasso and Braque: Pioneering Cubism*,
The Museum of Modern Art, New York, Little, Brown and
Company, Boston, 1989, ill. p. 261.

Zervos, Christian, *Pablo Picasso: Oeuvres de 1912 à 1917*,
Vol. II, part II, Edition Cahiers D'Art, Paris, p. 192, #409.

"The drawing of this violin, before it received its collage
elements, can be seen in photograph no. 1 of the Boulevard
Raspail studio (see Documentary Photographs). This
violin recurs in 535/PD." (Daix, p. 290)

6. **Femme Assise dans un Fauteuil** 1920

Oil on canvas

51.38" x 35.25" · 130.5 x 89.5 cm

Signed and dated lower right "Picasso '20".
This work was begun in Montrouge in 1917 and
completed in Paris in 1920.

PROVENANCE

Succession Picasso
Marina Picasso (inv. no. 12244, certificate no. 8001460
AB/03)
Private Collection, USA

EXHIBITED

Munich, Haus der Kunst, "Pablo Picasso, Werke aus der
Sammlung Marina Picasso", February–April 1981, ill. p.
297, #122; The exhibition also traveled to: Cologne, Josef-
Haubrich-Kunsthalle, August–October, 1981; Frankfurt,
Stadtische Galerie, October 1981–January, 1982; and Zurich,
Kunsthaus, January–March 1982.

Venice, Palazzo Grassi, "Picasso, Opere dal 1895 al 1971
dalla Collezione Marina Picasso", May–July, 1981, ill.,
p. 282, #174.

Tokyo, National Museum of Modern Art, "Masterpiece
from Marina Picasso Collection and from Museums in USA
and USSR", February–April, 1983, ill. in color p. 234,
#100. The exhibition also traveled to Kyoto, Municipal
Museum, June–July 1983.

Melbourne, National Gallery of Victoria, "Works from the
Marina Picasso Collection", July–September, 1984,
ill. p.76, #71. The exhibition also traveled to Sydney, Art
Gallery of New South Wales, October–December, 1984.

Paris, Artcurial, "Les Noces Catalanes", May–July, 1985,
ill. in color p. 49.

LITERATURE

G. Carandente (ed.), *Picasso, Opere dal 1895 al 1971 dalla
Collezione Marina Picasso*, G.C. Sansoni Editore Nuova,
Venice, 1981, ill. p. 282, #174.

W. Spies (ed.), *Picasso, Sammlung Marina Picasso*, Munich,
1981, ill. #122.

Zervos, Christian, *Pablo Picasso, Oeuvres de 1920–1924*, Vol.
IV, Edition Cahiers d'Art, Paris, 1951, p. 5, #14.

7. **Femme au Chapeau Tenant un Livre** 1921

Graphite on paper
42.52" x 29.53" · 108 x 75 cm

PROVENANCE

Ex-collection Marina Picasso (inv. 03094)
Daniel Varenne, Geneva
Richard Gray Gallery, Chicago
Private Collection, USA

LITERATURE

Carandente, G. (ed.), *Picasso, Opere dal 1895 al 1971 dalla
Collezione Marina Picasso*, Venice, 1981, p. 269, #149.

Zervos, Christian, *Pablo Picasso, Oeuvre Supplément aux
Années 1920–1922*, Volume XXX, Edition Cahiers d'Art,
Paris, p. 85, #260.

8. **Deux Danseurs** 1925

Pen and ink on paper
13.75" x 9.88" · 35 x 25 cm

Signed and dated lower right, "Picasso 25"

PROVENANCE

Richard Green Gallery, London
Richard & Mary L. Gray, Chicago

EXHIBITED

London, Richard Green Gallery, "XIX and XX Century
European Paintings", November 16–December 24, 1988, #29.

Osaka, The National Museum of Art, "Master Drawings -
Cezanne, Matisse, Picasso", October–November, 1989, ill. #7.

LITERATURE

Zervos, Christian, Pablo Picasso, Oeuvres de 1923 à 1925,
Volume V, Edition Cahiers d'Art, Paris, p. 175, #436.

9. **Tête** 1928

Oil and sand on canvas
21.5" x 12.85" · 55 x 33 cm

Signed upper left

PROVENANCE

Valentine Gallery, New York
Claire Zeisler, Chicago

EXHIBITED

Chicago, The Art Institute of Chicago, "Picasso in Chicago,
Paintings, Drawings and Prints from Chicago Collections",
February 3–March 31, 1968, ill. #32.

LITERATURE

Zervos, Christian, *Pablo Picasso, Oeuvres de 1926 à 1932*, Vol.
VII, Edition Cahiers d'Art, Paris, ill. p. 52, #121.

10. **Figure Etoilée** 1935

Oil on canvas
21.5" x 18" · 55 x 46 cm

Dated on stretcher "Paris 9 mars XXXV"

PROVENANCE

Galerie Louise Leiris, Paris (ref. 017910)
Galerie Patrice Trigano, Paris
Waddington Galleries, London
Private Collection, London
Richard Gray Gallery, Chicago

EXHIBITED

Venice Biennale, 1986

London, Waddington Galleries, "Pablo Picasso 1881–1973",
24 June–18 July, 1987, catalogue, ill. p.9, #3.

LITERATURE

Duncan, David Douglas, *Picasso's Picassos: The Treasures
of La Californie*, Harper & Row Publishers, New York, 1961,
p. 216.

Penrose, Roland, *Portrait of Picasso*, Published by The
Museum of Modern Art, New York, 1957, ill. p. 57, #145,
painting located on the left side of Picasso in a photograph
"Picasso in his studio, 7 rue des Grands Augustins", 1938,
photo by Peter Rose Pulham.

(Certificate of Authenticity, Maurice Jardot, Paris,
November 15, 1985.)

11. **Femme au Mouchoir et au Corsage Raye** 1937

Oil on canvas
21.5" x 15" · 55 x 38 cm

Dated on reverse "20 november 37"

PROVENANCE

Estate of the Artist
Private Collection
Richard Gray Gallery, Chicago
Acquavella Galleries, Inc., New York
Private Collection, USA

EXHIBITED

Chicago, Richard Gray Gallery, "Picasso's Picassos: Paintings, Drawings and Sculpture from the Artist's Estate",
April 3–May 9, 1985, ill. in color on cover.

Los Angeles County Museum of Art, "Picasso and the
Weeping Women: The Years of Marie-Thérèse Walter and
Dora Maar", February 10–May 1, 1994. The exhibition
traveled to: New York, The Metropolitan Museum of Art,
June 9–September 4, 1994, ill. in the catalogue p. 122,
fig. #85.

LITERATURE

Duncan, David Douglas, *Picasso's Picassos: The Treasures
of La Californie*, Harper & Row Publishers, New York, 1961,
ill. p. 226.

12. **Tête de Femme** ca. 1947

Oil on paper mounted on canvas
25.75" x 19.5" · 65.5 x 50 cm

Signed upper left

Galerie Louise Leiris, Paris
(#06722, photo #52930, November 8, 1947)

Schoneman Galleries, Inc., New York (1957)

Private Collection, Chicago

13. **Femme á la Veste Turque** 1955

Oil on canvas
51" x 38" · 130 x 97 cm

Signed upper left

PROVENANCE

Galerie Louise Leiris, Paris
Galerie Beyeler, Basel
Yayoi Gallery, Tokyo
Acquavella Gallery, New York
Paul Haim, Paris
Richard Gray Gallery, Chicago
Dr. and Mrs. LeRoy Pesch, Lake Forest, IL
Mr. Stefan Edlis and Ms. Gael Neeson, Chicago

LITERATURE

Leymarie, Jean, *Picasso Metamorphoses et Unités*, Skira, 1971, p. 176.

Zervos, Christian, *Pablo Picasso: Oeuvres de 1953 à 1955*, Vol. XVI, Edition Cahiers d'Art, Paris, p. 176, #527.

14. **Femme Nue Assise** 1959

Oil on canvas
57.5" x 45" · 146 x 114 cm

Signed and dated:
"14.2.59/18.2.59/19.22/8.-9.-3.-59" on reverse

PROVENANCE

Galerie Louise Leiris, Paris
Samuel M. Kootz Gallery, New York
Sally & Victor Ganz, New York
Richard Gray Gallery, Chicago
Private Collection, USA

EXHIBITED

New York, Samuel M. Kootz Gallery, "Picasso", 1962.

Toronto, The Art Gallery of Ontario; Montreal, Montreal
Museum of Art, "Picasso and Man", 1964, catalogue p. 151,
pl. #268.

New York, Cordier and Ekstrom, (Publication Associa-
tion), "Seven Decades of Modern Art", 1966.

Fort Worth, Fort Worth Art Center; Dallas, Dallas
Museum of Fine Arts, "Picasso", 1967, #79.

Baltimore, Baltimore Museum of Art, "Works from El
Greco to Pollock: Early and Late Works by European and
American Artists", 1968.

New York, Museum of Modern Art, "Pablo Picasso: A
Retrospective", 1980, ill. in the catalogue p. 435.

Paris, Musee National d'Art Moderne, "Le Dernier
Picasso, 1953–1973", 1988, # 17, ill. in color in the catalogue
p. 175.

London, The Tate Gallery, "Late Picasso", 1988, ill. in
color in the catalogue, p. 164, #11.

LITERATURE

Boggs, Jean Sutherland, "Picasso and the Nude", *Art News*,
Vol. 62, #9, January, 1964, pp. 29–30, fig. #8.

Duncan, David Douglas, *Picasso's Picassos: The Treasures
of La Californie*, Harper & Row Publishers, New York, 1961,
ill. p. 258.

Elsen, Albert E., *Purpose of Art*, New York, 1967, ill.
p. 390, #470.

Zervos, Christian, *Pablo Picasso: Oeuvres 1958 et 1959*,
Vol. XXIII, Edition Cahier d'Art, Paris, p. 89, #308.

15. **Nu Accroupi** 1960

Oil on canvas
57.5" x 44.9" · 146 x 114 cm

Signed lower left

PROVENANCE

Samuel M. Kootz Gallery, New York
Private Collection, Chicago

LITERATURE

Duncan, David Douglas, *Picasso's Picassos: The
Treasures of La Californie*, Harper & Row Publisher,
New York, 1961, ill. p. 258.

Zervos, Christian, Pablo *Picasso: Oeuvres de
1959–1961*, Vol. XIX, p. 44, #172.

16. **Tête Profile de Femme** 1960–1961

Cut out and painted sheet metal
11.5" x 10" x 3.25" · 29 x 25 x 8.5 cm

PROVENANCE

Estate of the Artist (inventory No. 56398)
Galerie 27, Paris
Private Collection, London
Richard Gray Gallery, Chicago

EXHIBITED

New York, NY, Barbara Mathes Gallery, "Sculpture, The
Figure Transformed", October 26–December 30, 1994.

LITERATURE

Pablo Picasso: Das plastische Werk, Werner Spies, Verlag
Gerd Hatje, Stuttgart, Catalogue No. 591A 2B, (illustrated
in b&w); exhibition traveled to Nationalgalerie Berlin,
Staatliche Museen Preussischer Kulturbesitz, October 7–
November 11, 1983; Kunsthalle Dusseldorf, December 12,
1983–January 29, 1984.

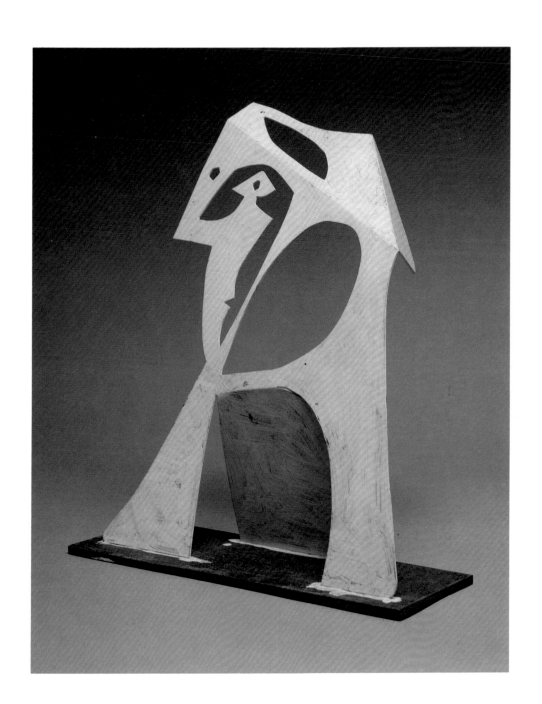

17. **Le Peintre et son Modéle** 1963

Oil on canvas

51.25" x 63.75" · 130 x 162 cm

Signed upper left

PROVENANCE

Galerie Louise Leiris, Paris
Galerie Krugier, Geneva
Collection Hans Schroeder, Garmisch-Patenkirchen
Private Collection, USA
Richard Gray Gallery, Chicago

EXHIBITED

Paris, Galerie Louise Leiris, "Picasso, Peintures 1962–63",
January, 1964, no. 36, illustrated pl. 35.

LITERATURE

Daix, P., Picasso, *l'homme et son oeuvre*, Paris,1964,
illustrated as dust-jacket.

Parmelin, Helene, *Le Peintre et son Modèle*, Paris, 1965,
ill. in color p. 154.

Zervos, C., *Pablo Picasso, Oeuvres de 1962 et 1963*, Vol.
XXIII, p. 190, #189.

18. **Enfant, Nu Agenouillé et Profile** 1969

Pencil on paper

19.88" x 25.59" · 50.5 x 65 cm

Signed upper right, "Picasso 4.9.69.II"

PROVENANCE

Galerie Louise Leiris, Paris
Saidenberg Gallery, New York
Private Collection, USA

EXHIBITED

Saratoga Springs, Skidmore College, February 18–
March 17, 1975.

Tubingen, Kunsthalle, "Picasso: Pastelle, Zeichnung,
Acquarelle", April 5–June 1, 1986, # 207. This exhibition
traveled to: Dusseldorf, Kunstsammlung Nordhein-
Westfalen, June 14–July 27, 1986, # 207.

LITERATURE

Spies, Werner, *Picasso: Pastelle, Zeichnungen, Acquarelle,
Verlag Gerd Hatje*, Stuttgart, 1986, ill. #207.

Zervos, Christian, *Pablo Picasso: Oeuvres 1969*, Vol. XXXI,
Edition Cahiers d'Art, Paris, p. 115, #405.